THE ART OF LIFE

How to Live a Happy and Meaningful Life

Minghao (Michael) HUANG, Ph.D.

Copyright © 2019 by Minghao Huang

All rights reserved. No part of this book may be reproduced, stored in a retrieval system, or transmitted in any form or by any means, electronic, mechanical, photocopying, recording, scanning, or otherwise, without the prior written permission of the publisher.

Disclaimer

All the material contained in this book is provided for educational and informational purposes only. No responsibility can be taken for any results or outcomes resulting from the use of this material.

While every attempt has been made to provide information that is both accurate and effective, the author does not assume any responsibility for the accuracy or use/misuse of this information.

For more information and other queries, please contact

mr.huangminghao@gmail.com.

Praise for MINGHAO HUANG's

The Art of Life

"… … *The Art of Life* is a wonderful book, I recommend it greatly, and it is a truly amazing book to help you if you are one of those many people having trouble dealing with life."

- Sophia X. ZHANG, *9-year-old girl who lives in Colorado*

"*The Art of Life* is an inspirational, philosophical, yet practical book. It provides a simple framework for the readers to follow and practice to achieve a happy and meaningful life. Minghao has amazingly combined insights and ideas from the classic books in the West and the East (the Bible and Tao Te Ching) and from business literatures, movies, and the emotional hardships he experienced as a child and as a young adult."

- Jing LI, *Professor of Simon Fraser University*

"With great wisdom, *the Art of Life* simplifies many profound and complex theoretical methods of personal transformation into five practical steps at a glance, which everyone can grasp and understand, so as to explore a happy and meaningful life step by step. *The Art of Life* is not only applicable to the exploration of individual family happiness, but also to social organizations and business management. What an outstanding book!"

- Shuxiang ZHANG, *A Reader*

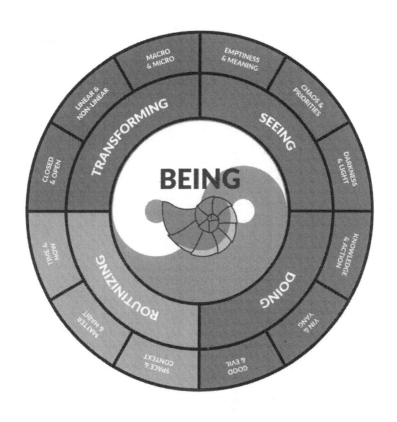

The Concept Map of the Art of Life

FROM BEING TO TRANSFORMING

STAGE ZERO: BEING

- How to Live a Happy and Meaningful Life?

STAGE ONE: SEEING

- How to Find the Meaning of Your Life?

- How to Design Your Priorities?

- What is Your Never-ending Engine?

STAGE TWO: DOING

- How to Manage Your Things and Relationships?

- What is Your Choice? Red or Blue Pill?

- How to Overcome Your Ethical Dilemmas?

STAGE THREE: ROUTINIZING

- What Determines Your Thoughts and Behaviors?

- How to Create Your Keystone Habit?

- How to Live Every Moment of Your Life?

STAGE INFINITY: TRANSFORMING

- How Transformation Occurs?

- How to Create a Golden Spiral in Your Life?

- Your Happy and Meaningful Life Matters!

With my deepest love,

this book is dedicated to my wife,

Sarah Hong,

and two beloved daughters,

Coco and Doa.

TABLE OF CONTENTS

A READER'S GUIDE FOR THE ART OF LIFE

The Master said: "Isn't it a pleasure to *study* and *practice* what you have learned? Isn't it also great when friends visit from distant places? If people do not recognize me and it doesn't bother me, am I not a noble man?"

- Confucius, *"The Analects of Confucius"*

Life is a journey with great adventures.

Before you start a new adventure to pursue your happiness without losing the meaning of your life, a guide for navigating the five stages of *the Art of Life* is needed to help you better practice what you will learn from this *SMALL* book.

First of all, *the Art of Life* is all about the way how to live *YOUR* life.

This book provides a simple, elegant, and beautiful pattern as a practical principle for anyone who wants to pursue a happy and meaningful life regardless of race, nationality, gender, and culture.

However, our individual life has its unique biological gene to selfishly pursue one's happiness, as well as the cultural context in which different perspectives, values, and meaning systems are emerged to interpret the purpose of your life in a completely different manner.

For this reason, *the Art of Life* has borrowed the original wisdom from two of the most widely translated and influential scriptures ever in human history: *the Bible* and *Tao Te Ching*. I have discovered the pattern from both scriptures, and the original numbers, sequence, and symbols are used to minimize the possible problems, confusion, and conflicts arose from different meaning systems of the east or west.

Finally, 0, 1, 2, 3, and ∞, as well as their significations, are used to form and structure *the Art of Life*. Correspondingly, this book is exclusively designed to have five building blocks, and each STAGE covers cutting-edge real-life questions that people desperately seek to answer nowadays.

To maximize your gains from *the Art of Life*, you are strongly recommended to empty your mind, be formless, shapeless — like water as Bruce Lee once advised. You'd better abandon your prejudice, stereotype, and discrimination against everything that is connected with your life, and be with *The Being*, at least, while you study and practice *the Art of Life*. It will help you to see your life from an entirely different perspective thereby seeing your life and the world as they are.

Only then, can all these numbers, symbols, and blocks become the music notes, and it's up to you, a great independent artist, to choose what kind of music you are going to compose with *The Being*. Every person has his or her unique rhythm of life melody, and no one can expect how beautiful a masterpiece you will create throughout *YOUR* life journey.

So, don't compare your unique life with others' nor live other people's experiences.

Second, you should read this book with your 3-H: Head, Heart, and Hands.

Although the physical distances from head to heart and again from the heart to hands are just about one cubit each, it is a time-consuming journey that takes life-long efforts to travel through. However, comparative to the way we see them linearly before, *the Art of Life* thinks that intellect, sensibilities, and will, which Head, Heart, and Hands represent, are out of one unified personal being. They are intertwined together to form the personality of an individual human being. So, this is going to be an experiential, intellectual, and spiritual adventure that calls for your whole body, mind, and soul.

To help you better practice it in your daily life, I provide a template of a practical guide at the end of each chapter so that you can apply *the Art of Life* to transform every aspect of your life. And what kind of problems, dilemmas, incidents, and challenges you choose to solve is entirely up to you.

Last but not least, *the Art of Life*, although it casts a shining light on how to live a happy and meaningful life, is merely another cubic block in your life. Since you can easily trap yourself in *the Art of Life* itself, you need to intentionally practice Being with *The Being* (will be interchangeably used with *Absolute Tao* and *I Am Who I Am* in this book), which are within and beyond *the Art of Life*.

When I got inspired and wanted to begin this project, I could not write a single word for quite a long time. The topic of how to live a happy and meaningful life is so huge that I was utterly overwhelmed. I knew that *the Art of Life* could not explain *Absolute Tao* or *I Am Who I Am* with the limited languages, but they are the most crucial component of *the Art of Life*.

It wasn't until I separate *The Being* from the main structure of this book in the form of STAGE ZERO, was I able to write it. I mean, *The Being* should be both transcendental from and incarnated within any cubic block, including *the Art of Life*. Thus, without STAGE ZERO, *the Art of Life* is incomplete.

I strongly recommend that you should finally learn to break out of *the Art of Life*, another cubic block, and live YOUR own happy and meaningful life by Being with *The Being*. That's what I hope for, and also the ultimate aim of *the Art of Life*.

All in all, please keep the reader's guide for *the Art of Life* in mind, and this *SMALL* book will help you live a happy and meaningful life.

- *YOUR* Happy and Meaningful Life Matters!

- Use Your Head, Heart, and Hands to Study and Practice *the Art of Life*.

- Live beyond *the Art of Life*.

MINGHAO (MICHAEL) HUANG

WEIHAI, SHANDONG

FEBRUARY, 2019

STAGE ZERO

ABSOLUTE TAO: I Am Who I Am

The Tao that can be told of,

is not *The Absolute Tao*;

The Names that can be given,

are not Absolute Names.

- Tao Te Ching, Chapter 1

God said to Moses, "*I am who I am.*

This is what you are to say to the Israelites:

'*I Am* has sent me to you'"

- The Bible, Exodus 3:14

The Absolute Tao and *I Am Who I Am* are the two Names in closest proximity to describe *The Being* that created all universe, including human being. Only with or within *The Being*, can we see every creature as they are, no more, no less. *The Art of Life* uses the absolute zero or the absolute coordinate origin as an analogy to *The Being* that cannot be told of, and *The*

Being is the alpha and omega of *the Art of Life*. STAGE ZERO is the very beginning of *the Art of Life*, and we have to learn first to be with *The Being* through meditation, pray, or breathing anytime, anyplace, and anyhow. This is the first and foremost prerequisite of *the Art of Life*.

The ART OF LIFE

How to Live a Happy and Meaningful Life?

Out of Tao, One is born; Out of One, Two; Out of Two, Three;
Out of Three, the Created Universe.

- Tao Te Ching, Chapter 42

In the beginning, God created the heavens and the earth. Now
the earth was formless and empty, darkness was over the
surface of the deep, and the Spirit of God was hovering over
waters. And God said, "Let there be light," and there was light.

- The Bible, Genesis 1:1~3

The art of life is of essential importance to every person no
matter rich or poor, man or woman, old or young, west or east,
because everyone wants to have a happy and meaningful life
but in vain to achieve both at the same time.

With an ongoing unprecedented technology revolution, human
beings are experiencing the complexities and uncertainties of
this changing turbulent world. To better deal with all these
emerging new challenges, wisdom is needed to embrace all the
significant aspects of human life.

Inspired by *the Bible* and *Tao Te Ching*, two of the most original and influential books ever, *the Art of Life*, then, has been developed and resolved into five status of existences. These are (0) Being (with *The Being*) ; (1) Seeing; (2) Doing; (3) Routinizing; and (∞) Transforming.

The *Absolute Tao* are *I Am Who I Am*, *The Being* of all Beings. *The Being* created the heavens and the earth, and human beings. Humans are beings by *The Being*, of *The Being*, and for *The Being*. Hence human beings will find a way home and shall not be wanted only when they are Being with *The Being*.

BEING with *The Being* means returning to zero because zero is both the end of all things and a new beginning for all possibilities. The wisdom of returning to zero is to empty everything in your mind, to free from everything that binds you, and to see all the created universe as it is. Thus, returning to zero is returning to *The Being*.

ONE is SEEING the meaning of all creation, especially the unique value of your own life. SEEING is discovering the meaning from the emptiness of your life, designing your priorities from a chaotic mess, and knowing that love is the never-ending engine of your growth. That's how Out of Tao, One is born.

TWO, Out of ONE. This implies the unity of all opposite dual structures such as knowing and DOING, zero and one, wave and particle, east and west, Yin and Yang, good and evil, life and death, heaven and earth, etc. In substance, dual structures are two sides of the same coin as wave-particle duality of light.

THREE represents ROUTINIZING the activities within a three-dimensional world where you live in. These are space, matter, and time, and they, as is well known, can be further divided into three different dimensions, states, and tenses. There is another corresponding three-dimensional world that is not visible, they are context, habit, and now.

Finally, INFINITY (∞) means TRANSFORMING through an open upward spiraling closed-loop. You can continuously be with *The Being* to continually renew your life at any moment. You will start anew where everything ends because where there is death, there is a new life. That's how transformation occurs.

Based on the feedback and reflections over both the current habit and the emerging new context, you should always be ready to return to zero. In this way, you could be with *The Being* anytime and initiate another cycle of the loop which forms a golden spiral. The Fibonacci spiral with golden ratio presents us a sustained growth path of life with an optimized size which permeates all structures, forms, and proportions.

These five components should be understood and practiced by

any person who wants to live a happy and meaningful life: he who knows and practices them will achieve both at the same time; he who knows them not will be quickly getting lost or trapped here and there.

In this sense, you can keep all the following questions in mind so that you can check if you are doing the right thing for the right people in a proper way at an appropriate time of your life.

- Do you know the idea of BEING with *The Being* by returning to zero at any moment?

- Did you SEE your calling to a particular cause, as well as specific purposes of your current life stage?

- Did you take some real ACTIONS to do meaningful things and build meaningful relationships?

- Did you identify and create the KEYSTONE HABIT of your life?

- Are you ready to continually return to zero by BEING with *The Being* so that you could continuously TRANSFORM your life?

If you want to learn and act upon it, and it really helps solve problems, dilemmas, incidents, and challenges, then, let it be integrated into your life. If you are not willing to learn nor act upon it, you might continue to search for the meaning and happiness of living in your own way, and then, let it be dismissed from your life.

As for the life trajectory, paradoxically, the Asians think the world is a circle, while Westerners think it's a line. However, *the Art of Life* claims that the world, as a grand living organic, shares a common growing pattern which is a spiral. Every life is born to grow, but the matter is increasing in what direction. Hence what makes *the Art of Life* so special is that it is forming an open closed-loop which helps your personal growth spiral upward.

All life stuff is based on *Absolute Tao* or *I Am Who I Am*, *The Being* of all beings. Hence, when you stop to be with *The Being*, you begin to see; when you know, you may have the courage to take actions; when you act, you can create a new habit; when you have a good habit, you will achieve your goals or have good virtues; with goals achieved and excellent virtues, you continually transform and grow; when you continuously transform and grow with the golden spiral, your life is bound to be both happy and meaningful no matter what circumstances you are in.

And this is *the Art of Life*, a simple, elegant, and beautiful pattern that can change your life. I hope you could enjoy this book!

STAGE ONE

Out of TAO, One is Born

Our life-purpose therefore comes from two sources at once -
who we are *created to be* and who we *are called to be*.

- Os Guinness, *"The Call"*

There is only one heroism in the world: to *see* the world *as it is*
and to *love it*.

- Romain Rolland

Out of Tao, One is born. This is a process of creation from zero
to one where you can SEE the meaning from emptiness, the
order from formless, and the light from darkness. The meaning
of life can be searched by SEEING your identity and locus as a
human being relative to the absolute coordinate origin, *The
Being* of all beings. Once done, you, then, can easily set up your
own priorities by further discovering the nature of everything
that is connected with your life. Finally, to live a happy and
meaningful life, you need a never-ending engine to energize
your life. That is love, a light that never dims nor fails.

EMPTINESS & MEANING:

How to Find the Meaning of Your Life?

Now, here is my secret, a very simple secret: It is *only with the heart* that one can *SEE* rightly; what is essential is invisible to the eye.

- Antoine Saint-Exupéry, *"The Little Prince"*

The way to find the meaning of life is just like the way the little prince saw a single flower blossom and grow in the vast sky. Because you have to find the meaning from the emptiness of your life which is like a handful of dust in the vast universe or a grain of sand in the deep desert. You cannot see it rightly with your eyes, but only with your heart, can you find the single, hidden, and true meaning of your own life.

In searching for the single meaning of your life, I am sorry to say that you cannot hire people to do the job. No one can help you find the meaning of your life instead, and you have to do it yourself. "Ultimately, man should not ask what the meaning of his life is," Viktor Frankl wrote in *Man's Search For Meaning (1946)*, "but rather must recognize that it is he who is asked. In a word, each man is questioned by life; and he can only answer to life by answering for his own life; to life, he can only respond by being responsible."

Life is unique one-way progress that is exclusively gifted to you, but you, as a life traveler, will often encounter "two roads diverged" along the way. Since you cannot travel both, according to Frankl, you may respond by keeping the "freedom to choose your attitude in any given set of circumstances, to choose your own way."

To choose your own way, you have to know yourself. Like Socrates said, *Man, know thyself!* In fact, knowing yourself is finding the ultimate meaning of your life, and the primary purpose of your life is unique to *The Being* which will help you get a higher level of "happiness" by answering all the following fundamental questions:

- Who am I?

- Where am I from?

- Why am I here now?

- Where I should go

- What do I live or die for?

- ... ...

Then, how to know yourself and find the meaning of your life?

To locate your position, you need a frame of reference or GPS. The meaning of your life is bound to be measured and determined by the frame you choose to follow. For some, the reason for living is all about making money. If you accept money as the pinnacle of your life, your life will be valued by how much you earn. If the most concern of your life is reputation, your happiness is calculated by how much honor you gain throughout your life. If you think the value of life comes from power, then, you will pursue symbols of power at any cost.

Popular as they are, money, reputation, and power are not the only choices you can make. A specific person, concept, or dogma, anything that you think of can provide you "a place to stand" so that you can "move the earth" by redefining everything according to the standard you choose to follow, as Archimedes once implied.

However, all these creatures have the fatal flaws of fleeting and fluctuating.

This is why *the Art of Life* addresses that the ultimate meaning of life can ONLY be searched by SEEING your identity and locus as a human being relative to the absolute coordinate origin, *The Being* of all beings which is the only perfect frame of reference that is constant and reliable. You could see your meaning of life with your heart by referring to *The Being*. That's how Out of Tao, The Meaning of Your Life is born.

The best way to demonstrate something abstract is to visualize it. So *the Art of Life* uses the coordinate system to help you better understand the way how to find the meaning of your life.

Before that, according to *the Call* authored by Os Guinness, *the Art of Life* divides the meaning into the primary meaning and secondary meanings: primary meaning is the response to the ultimate why and primary calling, while secondary meanings, as secondary callings, are matched with specific purposes at different life stages.

Let's SEE the primary meaning of your life, as it is created to be, which is determined by *The Being*.

Life is like sailing in the sea.

In the era of great navigation, people use the sextant to calculate the star angle. By SEEING the Polaris of the Big Dipper, you can locate latitude and longitude for yourself. Once the location is obtained, you can use the compass to plot the route on the map. In the same way, assuming that O is an absolute coordinate origin: *The Being*, you can identify the meaning of your life with the vector value of "You" from the source. Because vector value can be expressed in a direction (d) and the distance (v), you will have your unique vector OY determined by the absolute zero: the course and the value of your life.

Based on the primary meaning of your life, you can redefine everything that is connected with you, including the data you created, the things you have or do, the relationships you build, and the habits and virtues you cultivate. That is how the secondary meanings come into your life, and you need to SEE everything as they are called to be, which are exclusively customized for your own life.

Once you have the absolute coordinate origin, all the creatures that were fleeting and fluctuating begin to recover their original meanings of what they are created to be. For example, the essential definition of Money has a unique vector OM. One step further, you can identify what Money means to your life by adding the two vectors: $IM = OI + OM$. The direction here is critical because MI implies that you are determined by Money while IM, here, means that you decide the value of Money by referring to *The Being*: O.

In the same way, you can reidentify everything that is connected with you at the current stage of your life. However, secondary meanings will change according to your specific context at different life cycles, but they all have meanings as long as you are continually Being with *The Being*. Even if you cannot change any little decision you made before, the transcendental Being will renew the meanings of all your past life.

As a result, the existence of *The Being* gives all the creatures their original meaning and restores the order of creation. The identified primary meaning provides a cornerstone for your life, and you can prioritize everything that is connected with you, which will be discussed in the next chapter.

Sun Tzu once said in *the Art of War*: "If you know the enemy and know yourself, you need not to fear the result of a hundred battles," while *the Art of Life* advises: "If you know *The Being* and know yourself, you will have a happy and meaningful life whatever circumstances you are in." Because the better you know *The Being*, the better you will know yourself; and the better you know yourself, the better you will see *The Being*.

Before you move on to the next chapter, please follow the guide below and find your primary meaning and secondary meanings first so that you could get your Identity Map.

PRACTICAL GUIDE FOR FINDING THE MEANING OF YOUR LIFE

BEING: Being with *The Being* through meditation, prayer, breathing, etc.;

SEEING: See the fact that only *The Being* of all Beings can be a constant and reliable frame of reference to determine the meaning of your life;

DOING: Write down, visualize, and find the purpose of your life; Love your life as it is;

- Step 1: List primary meaning, relationships, things, habits, and virtues that are connected with your life;

- Step 2: Evaluate every item according to the actual frequencies of your interactions with them now by using five-point system (0: best, 1: great, 2: good, 3: average, 4: poor);

- Step 3: Based on the primary meaning of your life, you may re-evaluate each item;

- Step 4: Subtract the value of Step 3 from the value of Step 2, and you will get the list of gaps between as-is and to-be;

- Step 5: Visualize the four steps into the Concept Map to see your primary and secondary meanings at a glance. You may put your primary purpose at the center of the Concept Map, assign relationships to green quadrant, things to red quadrant, habits to yellow quadrant, and virtues to blue quadrant, and you get your Identity Map now.

ROUTINIZING: Create a habit of examining the meaning of your life with your Identity Map;

TRANSFORMING: Based on feedbacks and reflections, constantly return to zero and transform the secondary meanings of your life.

CHAOS & PRIORITIES:

How to Design Your Priorities?

You have to decide what your highest priorities are and have the courage—pleasantly, smilingly, non-apologetically, to say "no" to other things. And the way you do that is by having a bigger "yes" burning inside. The enemy of the "best" is often the "good."

- Steven Covey, *"Seven Habits of Highly Effective People"*

Designing your priorities means figuring out what you want most out of life and arrange these goals from most important to least critical.

One can hardly imagine a life without meaning and its priorities. If you don't have your own preferences, internal chaos takes on so many forms in your lives, and it can lead to the burnout of your mind and body. Do you find yourself automatically reacting to urgent and unimportant things prompted up on the screen of your smartphone? Are you mindlessly surfing on the internet and killing your precious time by chattering on SNS? Are you living another boring day without any life purpose that arouses your interests and passions? Do you ever have any experience of making some stupid decisions to buy something that you don't need at all? Are you the one who will never say "No" to other things and people that have nothing to do with the meaning of your life? And so on and on.

A profound shift is needed for the chaos within to be restored to order, and this can only be done when you are Being with *The Being* as has been mentioned in CHAPTER EMPTINESS & MEANING. In order not to live a chaotic life, you need to examine both the primary meaning and secondary meanings of your life with your Identity Map.

A significant paradigm shift is going on, and the way you design your priorities has to be fundamentally changed with it.

Before, people use the tree as an essential metaphor to identify the position of your body, mind, and soul from genealogy family tree, knowledge classification system, and religious symbols. However, the paradigm is shifting from tree structure to network structure. With the development of new technology, data, things, people, and processes are all connected into the Internet of Everything. Because of this, your identity can be easily identified with a user-friendly personal dashboard that shows all the indexes of the meanings, relationships, things, habits, and virtues very soon. However, drawing your Identity

Map manually can be a good starting point to understand the way how to design your priorities now.

Although experts say that paradigm is shifting from tree to network which has a decentralized and non-hierarchical characteristic, *the Art of Life* embraces both tree and network structures. As you have learned from CHAPTER EMPTINESS & MEANING, only when you know that *The Being* is the absolute original point where to rest upon, can you begin to SEE the primary meaning of your life. Once the direction and value of your life are determined, is it possible for you to know what is first and what is last in your life.

What's important here is that how you allocate your limited time resources to everything that is connected to your life reflects your current identity and value system. As a result, new time management tools are needed to help prioritize your relationships, things, habits, and virtues in each quadrant, and assign them into compatible time frames.

To do that, *the Art of Life* integrates dual roles of time, Chronos and Kairos, into developing a new generation of the time management framework. In case you first learn about the concepts of Chronos and Kairos, let's have a look at the metaphor Einstein used to illustrate the theory of relativity:

"Put your hand on a hot stove for a minute, and it seems like an hour. Sit with a pretty girl for an hour, and it seems like a minute. That's relativity."

- Albert Einstein

Einstein's analogy is so well known that you can easily understand the relativity of time, but few people realize that the relativity of time represents the dual identity of time hidden in this sentence.

Here, although Einstein used the same unit of time: minute and hour which appeared twice each, they did not mean the same time in fact. "Put your hand on a hot stove for a minute" and "sit with a pretty girl for an hour" are objective and continuous concepts of time that can be measured by calendar and clocks, which is called Chronos. And "it seems like an hour" and "it seems like a minute" are subjective, conscious and non-continuous concepts of time that can only be perceived by your heart, which is called Kairos.

For example, your full schedule, appointments at what time to meet who, and deadlines for a project all belong to Chronos, while the moments filled with beautiful memories that you will never forget and that make your heart start to jump again belong to Kairos.

Now, from the Identity Map you have drawn, you might easily find some overlaps between the stages and categories assigned to each quadrant.

That is to say, Kairos which has subjective, perceptive, and discontinuous characteristics play a more significant role in SEEING and TRANSFORMING, while Chronos which has an objective, quantitative and continuous characteristics plays a more substantial role in the DOING and ROUTINIZING. BEING encompass both concepts.

Then, how to design your priorities based on your Identity Map and what is the new generation of time management framework?

Your priorities should be synchronized with those of nature.

The big story of Scripture has creation, fall, redemption, and new creation. Everyone has birth, senility, illness, and death, and a year has spring, summer, autumn, and winter. A month has new moon, first quarter, full moon, and last quarter, and a day has sunrise, noon, sunset, and night.

So, you can align your biological clock with natural clock, and assign different stages to relevant time frames by Being with *The Being* every day. You'd better see the meaning of your day before sunrise, do first things first and manage your differential relationships till noon, routinize the actions till sunset, and transform yourself through reflections over your day at night. You don't have to follow this order mechanically, and I hope you could understand the spirit of the priorities.

Now you can choose the highest priorities from the list of each quadrant, and practice them every day with the practical guidance provided at the end of this chapter. You can also practice this monthly, yearly, and even within your whole life span, but the highest level of designing your priorities is that you can dynamically prioritize at any moment of your life.

Then you can align the colors, stages, categories, and time frames now so that you can design your priorities by Being with *The Being*, which is at the center of your life.

Before you move on to the next chapter, please follow the practical guide below to design your priorities so that your life can be flowering seasonally.

PRACTICAL GUIDE FOR DESIGNING YOUR PRIORITIES

BEING: No matter how important or urgent the thing is, learn to stop and put down the work at hand, and Be with the Being;

SEEING: Discover or confirm your priorities of the current stage of your life from each quadrant of your Identity Map and perceive the inherent needs of things and relationships you encounter now;

DOING: Design your priorities at that moment and then do

meaningful things and build meaningful relationships to satisfy their inherent needs;

ROUTINIZING: Make the three steps into a habit of improvising your priorities of relationships, things, habits, and virtues;

TRANSFORMING: Constantly return to zero and redesign your priorities based on new situations and your up-to-date Identity Map.

DARKNESS & LIGHT:

What is Your Never-ending Engine?

I'm stuck. It's dark. I'm overwhelmed.

I know what it's like down here, and you're not alone.

- Brené Brown on *Empathy*

Who is John Galt?

This question, as the opening line of Ayn Rand's novel *Atlas Shrugged (1957)*, repeatedly appeared in her book. Obviously, the author was using this question and the character, "John Galt," to deliver her most important message of rational individualism.

"My philosophy, in essence, is the concept of man as a heroic being, with his own happiness as the moral purpose of his life, with productive achievement as his noblest activity, and reason as his only absolute."

- Ayn Rand

From her most important confession in the appendix of the

novel, we can identify that what Ayn Rand concerns most is the "engine" that drives this world and keeps it progressing. From Ayn's individualistic philosophical framework, the "engine" is the inalienable right of individuals to use their minds solely for their own happiness with absolute reason and noblest activities. Her philosophy has inspired individuals around the world, and also profoundly impacted generations of American people so that they could discard norms and conventions to pursue their happy lives.

Just as the money, power, and reputation that have been mentioned in CHAPTER EMPTINESS & MEANING, reason can also be one of the most strong reference systems. However, although the rationality of human beings is the best engine to pursue your real happiness, it is also born to be limited in seeking a higher level of happiness: the meaning of your life. It seems that you are making your own decisions with your greatest deliberations, but you will finally see that the decision is not caused by your own free will. No matter what, you are trapped in a particular context which determines your thoughts and behaviors, and, in most cases, you cannot even tell which one is the result of your own reason. Then, how can one, who is not so-called an elite or a superman, rely on his bounded rationality or limited reason to pursue his happiness and meaning of life at the same time?

As you can see, if the reason is someone's only absolute, A.I. can perform much better than human beings because A.I. has an undeniable logic which you will learn in CHAPTER YIN & YANG. However, as Richard Nisbett, a professor of psychology at the University of Michigan and one of the world's most respected psychologists, wrote in *Chapter One: The Syllogism and The Tao of his book, the Geography of Thought*, "(Chinese) Dialectical thought is in some ways the opposite of logical thought. It seeks not to decontextualize but to see things in their appropriate contexts: Events do not occur in isolation from other events but are always embedded in a meaningful whole in which the elements are constantly changing and rearranging themselves," logic is not the only way of people to think and behave. Obviously, since reason cannot be the absolute reference framework that can determine the meaning and priorities of your life, let's call for a never-ending engine that is limitless, constant, and inexhaustible.

Instead of searching for the "engine" that drives this world, *the Art of Life* concerns more about the "engine" that drives your ordinary and excellent life. Because your happy and meaningful life does matter, and every average person's potentials could be ignited to make this world a better place to live. It seems that *the Art of Life* goes more in-depth to be individualistic, but it would be safer as long as you meet the primary prerequisite of *the Art of Life*: Being with *The Being*.

Yes! When you are Being with *The Being*, you are not merely a heroic being, and you are more than that. Romain Rolland provides the definition of true heroism with the following quote which I love most:

"There is only one heroism in the world: to see the world *as it is* and to love it."

- Romain Rolland

As a matter of fact, the confession of Ayn Rand contains all the essential elements of *the Art of Life*. It is merely an example of various applications of this simple, elegant, and beautiful pattern. Let's see her words from the perspective of *the Art of Life* as they are, and love it. Heroic Being, Seeing his own Happiness as the moral purpose of his life, Achieving (Doing) productively with his noblest activity (Routinizing, Virtues), and Transforming oneself through absolute reason (*Absolute Tao*) cover all the five stages. The difference comes from two different engines: one is the reason, the other is *The Being*. We can only say, the reason can be one of your secondary meanings at a particular stage of life, but never can be the primary meaning of your whole life.

To help you better understand what the "engine" of life is, let's break it down into a series of more specific questions:

● What drives your children to wake up early in the morning

to go to school?

- What motivates you to work hard for your goal even when all the people around you say you can't?

- What arouses your most interests and passions for a particular cause?

- What drives you to live and die for only one thing that really means to you?

- What drives entrepreneurs to explore new adventures and opportunities despite the tremendous potential risks they have?

From Daniel Pink's New York Times best-selling book, *Drive: The Surprising Truth About What Motivates Us*, we can find some fascinating findings on this topic. Daniel discovers that you should use different rewarding system toward two different kinds of work: a task using only mechanical skills and a job requiring more complicated, conceptual, creative thinking know-hows. Again, this coincides with the new generation of time management frame introduced in CHAPTER CHAOS & PRIORITIES. Since our mechanical work has been replaced by robots at high speed, the second type of work is more and more in need. When you do a creative job, in Daniel's theory, you need three factors that lead you to better performance and your personal satisfaction: autonomy, mastery, and purpose.

For our children, you can't imagine how you could drive them to study hard by using the primary meaning of life or three factors. For a certain age, a laptop, a bicycle with infinite gears, a baseball bat and glove, or a pair of fancy running shoes can motivate them better. Nevertheless, I don't want to set any boundaries on age when applying different motivation frameworks to them, because children are born to be creative and full of imagination.

It's not essential to use a specific motivation skill or another anymore. What matters most is to find the engine that can help you better understand the inherent needs of yourself and your differential relationships. To achieve that, you have to return to zero and see the unmet needs of your stakeholders with your heart and the power of empathy.

Whether you admit it or not, ever since the universe created, all creatures need energy to move, to live, and to be as they are created to be. There seems to be an invisible engine that is driving this world, and, in general, the original physical energy comes from light. Now that the natural light can be the source of energy which can dispel darkness and hold the whole universe in balance, you can still find a spiritual light that can shine in the shade of your heart and provide endless energy which can ignite your passions toward your empty life.

That is love, a light that never dims nor fails.

You might be stuck in tragedies of your life, and there is no strength to move a step forward; Your life could be in complete despair, and you cannot see any hope within darkness; Your heart might be completely frozen after being harmed by the people who you love and trust most.

Whatever circumstances you are in, you need an alternative force to help you free from any harsh situation in which you are trapped. According to Newton's first law of motion, you will continue with the current pace and direction unless something else causes you to change it. Only through the force of love in the presence of *The Being*: can you transcend your inner motivation to see the meaning of your life from emptiness; can you ignite the light of hope in despair and darkness; can you dissolve the frozen heart with the act of true love.

The American 3D animated fantasy film, *Frozen*, produced by Walt Disney Animation Studio, has given me unlimited imaginations and inspiration on this theme. *Frozen* not only gave me a great surprise in the 3D production technology but also in the plot settings and arrangements.

What impressed me most was that the final rescue of Anna's true love was not the Kiss of True Love which we took for granted, and it turned out to be the Act of True Love. When Anna saw Christopher is running to her, she abandoned the opportunity of saving her own life with the Kiss of True Love from him. Instead, to keep her sister Elsa, who was in danger, Anna chose to block the sharp sword with her dying body. The Act of True Love from Anna finally dissolved the frozen heart of Elsa, as well as the frozen world.

The two lines in the film best convey the meaning of the Act of True Love. One is what Alof says to Anna: "Putting someone else's needs before yours"; and the other is Elsa's last words, "You sacrificed yourself to save me?"

Similarly, the same message is conveyed in another 3D computer-animated musical adventure film, *Moana*, in 2016. In the movie, the heart of Te Fiti which Moana and Maui who vowed to return to Te Fiti should be the heart of true love.

The return of the heart of true love was finally accomplished by Moana's Act of True Love. At the end, when Moana realized that the demon Te Ka was the Te Fiti who lost her heart of true love, she risked her life and gently touched the forehead of Te Ka. The act of true love by Moana calms down the fire of wrath and Magna within Te Ka and finally restored to its original Te Fiti's beautiful appearance who could create new life again. The movie implies that anyone who loses the heart of true love could be a demon, and we can also be the one if we don't have the Act of True Love.

So only with true love, can you have the power of empathy to understand the sufferings of yourself and your differential relationships. Then, You have the engine to stop and put down everything you have, go downstairs, and say:

I know what it looks like below, you are not alone.

The act of true love comes from Seeing the meaning and priorities of your life, and it also leads to the topic of STAGE TWO, which is DOING. Before you move on to the next stage, please follow the practical guide to find your never-ending engine and review the three topics of STAGE ONE.

PRACTICAL GUIDE FOR FINDING YOUR NEVER-ENDING ENGINE

BEING: When you are stuck in the darkness or in despair, return to zero by praying, meditating, or breathing; Being in the presence of love that never dims nor fails;

SEEING: Observe the pains and tragedies as they are, and accept them; See the meaning of your life doesn't change whatever circumstances you are in; See the fact that you are created to be loved by the presence of *The Being*;

DOING: Take courage to move a small step forward so that you could achieve a small win to regain confidence; Live as if you are living a second life, then you fear nothing but give up;

ROUTINIZING: Create your keystone habit of making a small

step forward to achieve the small win, and never give up till it completely changes your situations and your whole life;

TRANSFORMING: Based on the feedback and reflections, make love as a never-ending engine or energy to make your life grow with the golden spiral, and never stop returning to zero to start again where you fell down.

STAGE TWO

OUT OF ONE, TWO

What I really need is to get clear about what I must do, not what I must know, except insofar as knowledge must precede every act. What matters is to find a purpose, to see what it really is that God wills that I shall do; the crucial thing is to find a truth which is truth for me, to find the idea for which I am willing to live and die.

- Journals of Søren Kierkegaard Entry, 1835

The highest good is the original substance of the mind. When one deviates a little from this original substance, there is evil. It is not that there is a good and there is also an evil to oppose it. Therefore good and evil are one thing.

- Wang Yangming

Two, Out of One. This implies the unity of all opposite dual structures such as knowing and DOING, zero and one, wave and particle, Yin and Yang, good and evil, life and death, heaven and earth, east and west, etc. In substance, dual structures are two sides of the same coin just as light has wave-particle duality.

WAVE & PARTICLE:

How to Manage Your Things and Relationships?

It was the best of times, it was the worst of times,

it was the age of wisdom, it was the age of foolishness,

it was the epoch of belief, it was the epoch of incredulity,

it was the season of Light, it was the season of Darkness,

it was the spring of hope, it was the winter of despair,

we had everything before us, we had nothing before us,

we were all going direct to Heaven, we were all going direct the
other way.

- Charles Dickens, *"A Tale of Two Cities"*

Among panda, monkey, and banana, consider which two of these objects go together?

When I taught the chapter of worldwide learning, innovation, and knowledge management in my international business class, I always start with this simple question by showing a picture of them. The test is one typical example of numerous experiments from the book, *The Geography of Thought*, by Richard Nisbett. I will not hesitate to say that this book will be your best choice if you want to understand how Asians and Westerners think differently and why.

Typically, students from Asian countries tend to choose the monkey and the banana more, because they are more likely to see this world from harmonious relationships or broader context; while students from West, who are more independent and individual, will pair the panda and the monkey more, merely because they are sharing the same feature of animals.

Of course, some outliers choose the other way entirely or even pick panda and banana by chance, but the vast majority of students prefer this way, which means that the difference of cognitive or knowledge systems under different cultural backgrounds does exist. The various cognitive and learning schemes, cultures, frames, and civilizations constructed by different perceptions and thinking habits lead to significant differences on many issues such as settling disputes, making our daily decisions, and the way to evaluate a person.

The most profound influence of this discrepancy is a series of exciting questions raised by Richard Nisbett in the epilogue of his book: The end of psychology or the clash of mentalities? In other words, "the end of history" by Francis Fukuyama or "the clash of civilizations" proposed by Samuel Huntington; Where are we headed? The convergence of two cognitive systems into one or a continued divergence of different cultures?

The west and east are just like the two cities in Dickens' novel which represent the duality between England and France. All these questions emerged when the Two comes Out of One: Best versus worst, wisdom versus foolishness, belief versus incredulity, light versus darkness, hope versus despair, everything versus nothing, heaven versus hell. Thus, you can think the other way around, the relationship between context and feature reflects the unity of all opposite dual structures such as knowing and DOING, zero and one, wave and particle, Yin and Yang, good and evil, life and death, heaven and earth, east and west, etc. In substance, all dual structures are two sides of the same coin just as light has wave-particle duality.

So, the relationship between context and feature reflects the wave-particle duality of light.

Interestingly, Business (*shengyi*) in Chinese character means creating meaning, while *zongheng* means vertical and horizontal. How to manage your things and relationships is about *zonghengshengyi* which means do meaningful things vertically and building meaningful relationships horizontally to cope with the sophisticated beauty of the network.

As the first chapter of Stage Two, it is the extension of Stage One and strongly coincides with the three main topics of it:

meaning, priorities, and light. This chapter tries to organically integrate the Western values of pursuing personal achievements and the Oriental values of seeking harmonious relationships into one meaning system which determines your own happiness, as well as the meaning of your life.

People used to focus too much on how to do things better by neglecting the valuable relationships they have. In modern society, what you know will determine your performance, while who you know is just your emotional relationships that have nothing to do with the key performance index of your job.

However, since Klaus Schwab declared that human beings were about to face the baptism of the Fourth Industrial Revolution, people were convinced that, shortly, human beings would experience a shocking experience and tremendous change in all fields. The chaos and uncertainty caused by this colossal transition cannot be comparable to the social change brought about by the industrial revolution described by Charles Dickens in his book: A Tale of Two Cities.

One of the most significant characteristics of the phenomena brought about by this new industrial revolution is that the emergence of revolutionary technologies such as robotics, A.I., nanotechnology, quantum computing, biotechnology, the Internet of Everything, 5G, and so on. What's more, the cultivation of a new urban civilization characterized by a smart city where all people, things and data, and processes are connected, lead to the crises and even collapse of existing systems, norms, rules, standards, habits and knowledge.

The way to manage your things and relationships is fundamentally changed into the form of creating meaning vertically and horizontally.

Based on the priorities you have drawn from your up-to-date Identity Map, you can put first things first and prioritize your differential relationships daily. You can build meaningful relationships by doing meaningful things, or you can do meaningful things by building meaningful relationships, and they are mutually reinforcing each other.

From the knowledge management perspective, the way to manage your things and relationships is also the way to create new knowledge beyond the east and west. Your life is composed of both your human capital and social capital, and you need to create new knowledge vertically and horizontally so that it can help you live a more happy and meaningful in this new era.

Then, how to equip yourself with such a knowledge engine to continuously create new knowledge?

Professor Ikujiro Nonaka, a renowned international knowledge management theorist, has a very classic paper on the spiral of knowledge creation. It is so valuable that he has transformed the academic achievements accumulated over the years into such a book, *Knowledge Flow*, co-authored with Ryoko Toyama and Toru Hirata.

To understand the spiral of knowledge creation, you must first understand the two categories of knowledge. Just as time is divided into visible Chronos time and invisible Kairos time, knowledge is also divided into visible "explicit knowledge" and invisible "tacit knowledge." The so-called explicit knowledge is the knowledge that can be readily articulated, codified, accessed and verbalized. For example, manuals, textbooks, documents, databases, procedures, etc. While Tacit knowledge is a kind of experience that can hardly transfer to another person through explicit instruction. For example, the ability to drive, play a musical instrument, speak a language, or manage a complex project.

The spiral of knowledge creation, also known as the SECI model, is realized through the mutual transformation between tacit knowledge and explicit knowledge. To illustrate the spiral of knowledge creation more vividly, I want to use the process of developing *the Art of Life* as an excellent example. The process from tacit to explicit, from 0 to 1: the idea that has been discovered through my own life experience and years of research was Externalized as a documented eBook, *the Art of*

Life. From explicit to explicit, the process from 1 to 2: based on the documented book, new explicit knowledge can be formed through Combination with a paper book and audiobook. From explicit to tacit, the process from 2 to 3: this is a learning process of Internalization through which you can make *the Art of Life* as your own tacit knowledge through study and practice. From tacit to tacit, from 3 to infinite or return-to-zero process: we have formed a community to interact with each other based on online and offline so that you learn by what you regularly see what I do and hear what I say.

In this way, the spiral of knowledge creation overlaps entirely with the golden spiral of *the Art of Life*. However, this is just about how to manage your things from a knowledge management perspective.

Now, let's discuss how to build and manage your essential relationship network.

The relationship has its own characteristics and differentials according to different essential factors, such as distance and closeness, strength and weakness. This difference comes from the following two dimensions: strong tie versus weak tie and sentimental relationship versus instrumental relationship. The strong tie or weak tie can be judged by the frequency of contact, while the sentimental or instrumental relationship can be differentiated on the basis of following relationship construction, that is, instrumental relationship if it is based on contractual arm's length relationship, and sentimental relationship if it is based on consanguinity or other emotional affinities.

According to two dimensions mentioned, we can construct four quadrants. These four quadrants represent differential relationships that you may encounter at different stages of your life. These relationships are all critical to you, but in various stages and situations of life, the priorities of these relationships may be different accordingly.

The interest-oriented weak relationship in the first quadrant is also called as strangers with Weak Tie, which is very famous for its strength proposed by Mark Granovetter, a very eminent American sociologist and professor at Stanford University. Because much valuable information such as employment opportunities are achieved through this first quadrant relationship.

The interest-oriented strong relationship in the second quadrant refers to colleagues and partners. As a mixed relationship, it is also the most difficult relationship to manage. You should not only invest your emotional inputs but also have sufficient contractual formal relationships to prevent opportunism.

The third quadrant is the weak relationship with emotional orientation. For men, it is a gentleman's acquaintance; while for women, it is a bestie. Because of the burdens from work and life, although you can't keep in touch with each other frequently, they are always ready for your call out and have a long talk even at midnight.

The fourth quadrant refers to the kinship quadrant based on blood ties. Similarly, the blood ties established from the emotional demand law constitutes a solid foundation for family businesses in the East and the West. Especially in the East, such as blood ties, geographic ties, academic ties, and military ties often play a decisive role. In the West, these relationships also play a crucial role, but the individualistic tendency of Westerners' independence weakens this relationship slightly.

Although we have four different types of relationships, each one requires time and effort, and the rules governing those relationships are different. However, each of us has limited time and resources. You can't spend all your time on your emotional connections so that people will become idle; You can't focus all your resources on the weak tie of interest orientation so that you will become snobbish people who are unacknowledged by your strong relationships.

You must manage these important relationships by investing different resources and principles in building a meaningful network of contacts, according to different types of relationships, your own life values, and current specific goals.

Finally, in the process of building network relationships, there is also some structural factor that plays a vital role. Especially for those who want to start a business or exert influence, they want to use their limited resources to build the maximized network influence.

To this end, you need to understand the following concept: Structural Holes. Generally speaking, structural holes, like acupoints in our human body, are essential nodes connecting different isolated networks.

The formal systems of the West are relatively more developed, and individual freedom or independence is more respected and emphasized. In this context, weak ties can connect different groups or people who are isolated from each other at a lower cost. That is to say, the benefits of Structural Hole can cover a broader range and obtain non-redundant information from different groups or people, which can not only improve the chances of profit-seeking but also increase the chances of organizational change and innovation. This is the strength of weak ties that have been mentioned above.

On the contrary, in the East where informal institutions are still playing their more significant roles and collective agency or harmony is more valued, the guanxi is based on strong ties such as affiliation, geography, and personal interaction experience. Only in such a closed and sticky relationship can members be willing to share valuable information and obtain intermediary interests. We call it the strength of strong ties.

Then, in the process of building your meaningful relationship network, you can refer to the following essential aspects. Firstly, based on the two dimensions mentioned above, you may draw your Identity Map and correctly determine the type of relationship with people, things, habits, and virtues. Secondly, based on the primary value of your life and your specific goals of the current stage of life, you may accordingly allocate your limited time and resources to those different groups that are meaningful to you. Finally, under the same conditions, you are recommended to build strong relationships with the person who has the highest centrality in different groups. The network you have formed like this is called the entrepreneurship network, that is to say, such a network combines the strength of strong ties with the power of weak ties, to maximize their social capital.

Of course, to build such an entrepreneurship network, you first need to learn and grow vertically, and you also need to have enough ability to maintain such a meaningful system of relationships.

Again, doing meaningful things and building meaningful relationships will mutually reinforce each other and forms a golden spiral of your personal growth. Please follow the practical guide to create new knowledge with a golden spiral by doing meaningful things vertically and building meaningful relationships horizontally every day.

PRACTICAL GUIDE FOR CREATING NEW KNOWLEDGE WITH GOLDEN SPIRAL

BEING: By returning to zero, Empty your mind, be formless, shapeless; Stay hungry and stay foolish;

SEEING: Discover that things and relationship, text and context, west and east, explicit and tacit knowledge share the same structure of duality of knowledge, as light has a wave-particle duality;

DOING: Create meaning and new knowledge by DOING meaningful things vertically and BUILDING meaningful relationships horizontally;

ROUTINIZING: Create a keystone habit of doing meaningful things and building meaningful relationships every day.

TRANSFORMING: Constantly return to zero to mutually reinforce each other so that you could grow with a golden spiral every day.

YIN & YANG:

What is Your Choice? Red or Blue Pill?

This is your last chance. After this, there is no turning back. You take the blue pill - the story ends, you wake up in your bed and believe whatever you want to believe. You take the red pill - you stay in wonderland and I show you how deep the rabbit-hole goes.

- Morpheus, *"Matrix"*

This is the choice offered by the rebel leader Morpheus to the main character Neo, in the film of *Matrix (1999)*.

Neo has to make a crucial decision to choose either an uncertain future with a meaningful "truth of reality" or a beautiful prison with blissful ignorant happiness. The dilemma reminds me of a tricky poem, *The Road Not Taken*, written by Robert Frost. Neo is standing in front of the "two roads diverged in a yellow wood, and sorry he could not travel both."

Since then, the red pill and the blue pill become a popular cultural meme or a metaphor, which represents the choice between real life and the virtual world. Desperate freedom and the brutal truths of reality which is represented by the red pill or the blue pill which symbolizes a life of luxurious security, tranquil happiness and the blissful ignorance of illusion.

Then, if you were Neo, what will you choose?

It will be one of the toughest decisions you will ever make because whichever pill you choose, you're sure to miss something good from selecting the other one. Personal happiness and the meaning of your life are equally important, but, from the perspective of either one or the other, it seems that you cannot achieve both at the same time. If this is true, *the Art of Life* doesn't need to exist.

However, the Chinese philosophy of yin and yang has a very different answer to this question. In ancient Chinese philosophy, Two, Out of One. This implies the unity of all opposite dual structures such as wave and particle, Yin and Yang, east and west, network and tree, AI and Human, evil and good, knowledge and action, informal and formal rules, tacit knowledge and explicit Knowledge, 0 and 1, dragon and phoenix, market and hierarchy, and so on.

The concept of dualism describes how seemingly opposite or contradictory forces may actually be complementary, interconnected, and interdependent in the natural world, and you cannot choose only one by neglecting the other. In fact, whatever choice you make, it contains both red and blue pills.

I still remember that I used to be at precisely the same situation as Neo when my parents decided to get divorced. At the age of seven years old, I have to choose between Dad and Mum. It's a tough decision then, but later I realized that whoever I wanted, I was not free from the influence of the other despite not seeing my Mum for over seven years. The experience helps me to understand better the relationship between Yin and Yang, as well as the fundamental principle of marriage which is the unity of a man and a woman.

In the same rationale, you can pursue a happy and meaningful life at the same time which used to be treated as different life-purposes. You may either find a reason to be happy in a meaningful "truth of reality" or anchor the meaning for the blissful ignorant happiness. What matters here is to see your own content and meaningful life based on who you are, i.e., the primary purpose and the secondary meanings of your life.

The world is fast changing and technology is advancing with it. Among those dualities of this world, one of the most significant challenges is from 0 and 1 two-digit digital world which has been evolved into A.I. You have to think about this question because everyone is "playing chess" with AlphaGo by using your smartphone now. The way how you interact with your smartphone determines the relationship between you and A.I.

Are you pursuing convenience at the cost of your privacy or personal data? What is your choice? Red or Blue Pill?

As humans, you are faced with a challenge to manage the relationship with the machine, A.I. and matrix. Rather than use technology to serve you, you have become the slave of this small gadget. You are living in your smartphone by neglecting all the real-life relationships. I mean you might be already living in the "Matrix" now.

Recalling the film, *Matrix*, you can easily see how technology is used to control and monitor humans with the latter being helpless in most cases. With *the Art of Life*, you no longer have to be a slave to technology but a proactive user like Steve Jobs who made inventions and innovate with technology. All these can happen if you implement 5 stages of *the Art of Life*: Being, Seeing, Doing, Routinizing and Transforming.

The evolution of the iPod, iPad, iPhone, and iMac will finally lead people to iRobot one day. The relationship between you and the machine has to be considered with institutional properties, and their relationships can be reflected from the recommended movies such as *Modern Times (1936)*, *Truman Show (1998)*, *Matrix (1999)*, and *I, Robot (2004)*. Human agents make technologies, and technologies not only influence one's thoughts and behaviors, but also change the institutional properties, and institutional properties determine one's thoughts and actions which will be introduced in CHAPTER SPACE & CONTEXT.

We are now also living in the city which has a smart brain, and everything is going to be connected with the internet. Our relationships, things, habits, and even your virtues can be connected or plugged in this network. If you are to identify yourself within the Internet of Everything, then the A.I. can better identify you.

Thus, the rights over personal data should return from big platform companies to every single human being, so that you can store, manage, and transact their precious assets with your free will. What' more important, you can use such kind of technology and personal data to manage your Identity Map visually and effectively. All the personalized service will be provided on your consent of using your personal data based on the value, meaning, and identity of your life. Thus, you need *the Art of Life* to manage the relationships between You, technology, and institutional properties which are the most essential relationships in this new era.

So, you have to ask yourself another question: Are you ready to play chess with AlphaGo? Please follow the practical guide to get prepared for it.

PRACTICAL GUIDE FOR BEING READY TO PLAY CHESS WITH ALPHAGO

BEING: Return to zero to be with *The Being*; Stop and put aside or turn off your smartphone so that you are in the presence of *The Being*;

SEEING: SEE the essence of relationships between you and smartphone; focus more on the meaningful relationships in your real life.

DOING: Consciously make your smartphone as a useful tool to help you live a happy and meaningful life; Recover your freedom not to reactively response to the pop-up messages, but proactively use your smartphone;

ROUTINIZING: Set up some rules and create a good habit of using smartphone first;

TRANSFORMING: Constantly return to zero, and learn to TRANSFORM yourself and redefine the essential relationship between you and the smartphone.

GOOD & EVIL:

How to Overcome Your Ethical Dilemmas?

Save him, and do what a doctor should do.

If it's necessary to kill him, I'll do it.

- Korean Drama, *"Descendants of the Sun"*

There is no era in which such a high moral requirement is imposed on a person or organization as it is now.

Governments are strengthening their anti-corruption efforts by enacting more stringent Anti-corruption and Bribery Prohibition Acts. Firms, especially multinational enterprises have to deliberately scheme their Corporate Social Responsibility (CSR) policies so that they could achieve both local presence and global sustainability by meeting the needs of different stakeholders in different cultures.

In such a world where various cultures and values conflict, individuals are trapped in the marsh and march of endless moral and ethical choices, unable to extricate themselves from them. As you can see from CHAPTER YIN & YANG, they are continuously oscillating between all opposite dual structures such as Yin and Yang, east and west, network and tree, AI and Human, good and evil, knowledge and action, informal and formal rules, tacit knowledge and explicit Knowledge, 0 and 1, market and hierarchy, and so on. Among them, good and evil are one of the most original and fundamental ethical dilemmas you have to face and overcome in your daily work and life.

What is right or wrong? What is the standard of good and evil? What is the underlying assumption on the nature of human beings: *Homo-economicus* that seeks self-interest or *Homo-sociologicus* that values altruistic behaviors more? How to choose between pursuing solely for their own happiness and seeking something meaningful bigger than themselves? The problem here is that you cannot find a compromise between good and evil to overcome the ethical dilemma.

Then, how to overcome your ethical dilemma in your daily work and life?

You might already get some insights from former chapters of this book. In CHAPTER CHAOS & PRIORITIES, you have learned that how you allocate your limited time resources to everything that is connected to your life reflects your current identity and value system. To overcome the ethical dilemma, you have to return to zero and find the meaning of your life first. You, as a moral agent, have to express who you are through all the decisions you make in your work and life, rather than based on self-interests or social norms. I mean, you need to make any decisions as a Being with *The Being*.

The meaning of your life can be divided into the primary purpose and the secondary meanings, and, in the Os Guinness' voice, they can be illustrated as "a life-purpose that comes from two sources at once - who we are created to be and who we are called to be." Most decisions you make have a direct relationship with who you are called to be, which is based on who you are created to be. You have to know thyself and find a constant, absolute, and reliable place to stand so that you will no longer be bothered by the ethical dilemmas of your life. Only then, can you build meaningful relationships, do meaningful things, create good habits, and cultivate noble virtues to live a happy and meaningful life that is created and called by *The Being*.

When I teach and discuss ethical dilemmas faced by MNEs with my students of International Business class, I have always been struggling to find an easy way to explain it. Not until one of my friends strongly recommended an animation that is related to this topic, did I stop searching for a better way for that purpose, because, as far as I know, it is one of the best works on moral and ethical issues.

Monster is an animation adapted from Naoki Urasawa's original comic book. The story is set in Germany and the Czech Republic after the fall of the Berlin Wall. The story shows the best and worst sides of human nature without any hindrance and provides extreme cases of ethical dilemmas throughout the whole story.

In the beginning, Dr. Tenma, a highly-talented Japanese brain surgeon, fell into a familiar ethical dilemma between the Turkish worker who had an accident but arrived hospital first and the famous vocalist Mr. Roshenbach who came to the hospital later. Although he knew it breached the code of doctor's conduct, he unwillingly obeyed the orders of the Directo Heinemann and saved the life of the vocalist accompanied by the death of the worker. Faced with the complaints of the worker's wife and their crying little son, although Dr. Tenma did it according to the director's instructions, he could not forgive himself and began to have grave doubt about the value of his profession as a doctor.

In the process of such a mental struggle, Dr. Tenma had the second chance to face the same ethical dilemma soon. This time, he had to choose between a boy, named Johan, who had a gunshot wound to his head and the Mayor Roedecker who arrived later. This time, Dr. Tenma decided to disobey the director's order and operated on Johan first instead of the mayor. Because Dr. Tenma did not want to use his refined medical techniques as a means of promotion and fame fishing, he wanted to hold a fair attitude towards all people's lives and to fulfill his duties to all patients as a doctor.

As a result, the mayor died, and the boy was saved.

Although Dr. Tenma paid a painful price for this choice, Dr. Tenma did not regret it. Until one day he found out that the boy he had saved desperately was the killing monster. He felt great responsibility for his choice and decided to chase and kill Johan with his own hands. A doctor who should save lives was planning to kill the boy whom he had rescued.

What a huge, dramatic setting it is!

However, the most extreme ethical dilemma came to Dr. Tenma at the end of this animation. When Dr. Tenma hesitated to pull the trigger, Johan was shot again by another person and fell down in front of Dr. Tenma. Another ultimate moral dilemma was encountered by Dr. Tenma: Do you want to operate on the monster you've been pursuing?

To my great surprise, Dr. Tenma once again saved the monster with his refined medical skills. When, as a monster, Johan slowly began to find his name and memory, and the story ended with the disappear of Johan, as well as the monster.

At that moment, I began to understand what is the critical

message that the author, Naoki Urasawa, would like to deliver through such a 74-episode anime TV series. The author gave us a profound insight into how you could overcome various ethical dilemmas in your work and life.

As a doctor, what Tenma could only do is what a doctor should do: save lives.

As a doctor again, Tenma could not judge whether the patient was an angel or a monster, or whether the patient was rich or poor, good or evil. He, as a doctor, should treat all lives equally and save at his best with his talented skills.

Let's take a look at a Korean drama, *The Descendants of the Sun*, to have s step further into this theme.

The plot is very talented. This work also chooses two extreme professions: doctors and soldiers. Through the love between the two heroes and heroines as the main line, it explores a lot of professional ethics and standards of good and evil.

I would like to use a scene similar to the end of the work, *Monster*, mentioned above to remind you once again about this.

Song Jong-Ki, as a soldier, let Song Hye-Kyo, a doctor, to save the gang leader who wanted to kill them by saying the following most impressive lines:

Save him, and do what a doctor should do.

If it's necessary to kill him, I'll do it.

Now, it's clear how you can overcome the ethical dilemmas in your daily work and life. If you want to be free from your struggles between good and evil, please follow the practical guide whenever you face your ethical dilemmas.

PRACTICAL GUIDE FOR OVERCOMING ETHICAL DILEMMA

BEING: When confronted by the ethical dilemma, stop and be in the presence of *The Being*, because the good and evil can only be determined by *The Being*;

SEEING: See what is the ultimate meaning and secondary meanings of your life, and identify the essence of the task and the role you should play in the specific context;

DOING: Do not judge good and evil, and do what you should do based on your Identity Map; If you do more than what you should do, you should be ready to take the responsibility of that intervention;

ROUTINIZING: Make it into a vocational habit; When you can't identify your role, please return to STAGE ZERO of this book, and learn the keystone habit of creating new habits, *the Art of Life*.

TRANSFORMING: Constantly return to zero, and continuously identify and live the meaning of your life.

STAGE THREE

OUT OF TWO, THREE

Remember then: there is only one time that is important — now! It is the most important time because it is the only time when we have any power. The most necessary person is the one with whom you are, for no man knows whether he will ever have dealings with anyone else: and the most important affair is to do that person good, because for that purpose alone was man sent into this life.

- Leo Tolstoy, *"The Three Questions"*

Empty your mind, be formless, shapeless — like water. Now you put water in a cup, it becomes the cup; You put water into a bottle it becomes the bottle; You put it in a teapot it becomes the teapot. Now water can flow or it can crash.

- Bruce Lee

Out of Two, Three. THREE represents ROUTINIZING the activities within a three-dimensional world where you live. These are space, matter, and time, and they, as is well known, can be further divided into three different dimensions, states, and tenses. There is another three-dimensional world that is not visible: they are context, habit, and now. It would be best if you learned to live within *the Being* to live beyond all the other cubes.

SPACE & CONTEXT:

What Determines Your Thoughts and Behaviors?

If you want people to be creative, you have to put people in an environment that lets their imagination soar. Most people experience "cubicle creativity": The size of their ideas is directly proportional to the space they have in which to think.

- General Haman, founder of *SOLUTIONSpeople*

Space and context are essential metrics that determine your behaviors and thoughts.

Everyone's body and mind at a particular time are in a certain space and context. Physically, you can easily perceive the area you are in and identify the location of yourself without any difficulties because GPS will kindly help you to do that job now. However, if you are only aware of the visible space and your physical location, you are ignoring the existence of invisible institutional context which, in most cases, plays a more decisive role than the physical one in determining your thoughts and behaviors.

In other words, if you understand the institutional context which is formed by three institutional forces, you can better understand the way how they determine your thoughts and behaviors. Further, you can also better create your keystone habit because habit, as a routine of social activities, is generally formed and imprinted by how you perceive and interact with these three forces: coercive, normative, and mimetic forces. These three forces are independent and also intertwined to form an institutional context. You have to know these forces and also learn how to deal with these different forces because every individual person has his own specific situation at a certain point of time.

Whenever I explain these three institutional forces and context, I like to use the traffic signal and cube as metaphors both of which readers are all familiar with.

The traffic signal has three colors: red, yellow, and green, and the three colors are representing the three institutional pressures. Every day, you are interacting with these three colors without noticing that these three colors are actually forming your travel habit. But if you take a moment to observe, you can easily find that they are everywhere, even in emerging new technology such as A.I.

Now, let's learn what these three omnipresent forces are and how they determine your thoughts and behaviors more specifically.

Red signifies the regulatory or coercive forces, such as laws, rules, and discipline. If you don't conform to them, you cannot survive. For example, if you don't obey the red light of the traffic signal, you will either lose your life, or get fined, or be disqualified from driving your car.

Yellow signifies norms and peer pressures. Though they don't' have a coercive force, it has even the higher power than the other two forces to influence the thoughts and behaviors of people. If everyone around you breaks the traffic signals, your chances of violating traffic signals with them will be significantly increased.

Finally, green represents cognitive or mimetic forces, such as culture and ethics. Mimetic forces lead you to two different directions: one is identification with extant culture by consciously conforming to it which makes you think and behave more identical with your cultural group people; the other is differentiation from your current culture by intentionally conforming to the norms or values of strategic groups so that your thoughts and behaviors will deviate from current rules. Because of this force, you can stop before the red light even when all your peer group people are violating it.

The three institutional forces are playing a role of assimilating your thoughts and behaviors to be identical with the institutional context you live in. If you don't follow the laws, norms, cultures, and ethical standards of the setting, you must leave because you don't have the legitimacy to live there.

All these three pressures are powerful, but, as has been mentioned above, norms and peer pressures, in a certain sense, have more power than regulatory power. Herding behavior is a typical example of this force. When everyone is sitting, you cannot stand alone; when everyone is saying yes, you cannot say no alone; when everyone is saying that you can't do it, you can hardly stick to what you are doing if you don't have enough belief to your goal.

That's why marketing strategists are designing various advertisements and campaigns to form peer pressures that push you to buy something that you don't even need on Black Friday. You buy them merely because your peer friends are buying them, but not because you are the one who really needs it. All the ads are telling one story: if you don't buy a product or service, you are just outdated. We are almost drowning in a sea of advertisements and marketing campaigns, and the peer pressures formed unconsciously by these ads are indeed the driving force to determine our shopping behaviors and habits.

If you carefully examine your thoughts and behaviors, you will find that there are no exceptional cases that are not influenced by these three forces. Again, if you don't follow institutional pressures, you have to leave. However, you have no place to escape because every unit has its coercive law, norms, cultures and ethical standards at different scales and levels.

Just like those actors who are moving between cubical rooms in the psychological horror thriller film series movie, *Cube (1997, 2002, 2004)*, you are prisoned in such a three-dimensional structure. In *Cube (1997)*, a small social group was formed by six people with different jobs: a prison escapist, a police officer, a mathematics student, a free clinic doctor, an architect, and an autistic savant. With a common purpose of escaping from this gigantic, mechanized cubical structure of unknown meaning and origin, principle characters representing different groups of people in real society are making decisions individually or collectively to escape from the cube. Deadly booby traps such as flamethrowers and razor-wire are playing a role as coercive forces that you cannot deny. Even in such a temporarily formed team, you can find norms, cultures, and ethics that influence their thoughts and behaviors. They are using all the skills and talents to avoid the traps and moving from one cubic to another by identifying their position and trigger mechanism of those traps, while also trying to solve the mystery of what the cube is and why they are in it. However, it finally turns out that their efforts to navigate out of the maze are actually "redundant" because they disappointedly discovered that the exit cube is the one from which they started this long journey. Finally, before the final escape, Worth (the architect) and Leaven (the mathematics student) had a dialogue on another ultimate dilemma: stay or leave:

Worth: I have nothing... to live for out there.

Leaven: What is out there?

Worth: Boundless human stupidity.

Leaven: I can live with that.

- Movie, *"Cube"*

However, by breaking everyone's expectations and assumptions, only Kazan (autistic savant) managed to escape the maze.

Although the movie can be interpreted in many different ways, *the Art of Life* thinks of a cube as space and context which determines your thoughts and behaviors. However, there is a difference between The Cube and cubes. The three-dimensional cube reminds me of *Trinity* in Christianity, as well as "Out of Three, The Created Universe" in *Tao Te Ching*. The Christian doctrine of *the Trinity* holds that God is the One but has three coeternal presences: *the Father, the Son (Jesus*

Christ), and the Holy Spirit; while *Tao Te Ching* also has a similar triad structure *Yin, Yang, and Qi*. The typical triad structure of *The Being* is *The Cube*, which determines the primary meaning of your life. All the other physical space and institutional context at different scales and levels are the cubes which decide on your secondary meanings. Now it's clear why triad structure is so omnipresent and determines your thoughts and behaviors. In order not to be trapped by any cubical room, you have to be in *The Cube* so that you could live beyond cubes. In other words, you have to be with *The Being* in order not to be determined by any different frame of reference which is fleeting and fluctuating.

You can find the three colors everywhere including logo designs of some big companies such as Google, Microsoft, Tencent, and Apple. The blue color symbolizes trust, loyalty, wisdom, faith, truth, and heaven which could connect all these three colors through transformation. That's how the Concept Map of *the Art of Life* is designed so that you are living beyond the institutional cubes (green, red, and yellow) but within *The Being* through continuous transforming (blue).

Now you can follow the guide to practice living beyond cubes that you cannot escape and within The Cube.

PRACTICAL GUIDE FOR LIVE BEYOND CUBES AND WITHIN THE CUBE

BEING: Empty everything in your mind, be formless, shapeless — like water;

SEEING: See the only way of being out of space and institution context is to be with *The Being*, The Cube, which determines the primary meaning of your life;

DOING: Accept the fact that you cannot escape space and context which defines your thoughts and behaviors, and live beyond them by continually returning to The Cube;

ROUTINIZING: Create a habit of adapting to and transforming all the artificial cubes by being within The Cube;

TRANSFORMING: Constantly return to zero, and transform your life, space, and context.

MATTER & HABIT:

How to Create Your Keystone Habit?

Sow a thought, and you reap an act;

Sow an act, and you reap a habit;

Sow a habit, and you reap a character;

Sow a character, and you reap a destiny.

— Samuel Smiles, *"Happy Homes and the Hearts That Make Them"*

In his New York Times Bestseller book, the Power of Habit, Charles Duhigg provides excellent insights to answer why we do what we do in life and business, and he illustrates a practical step-by-step guide to help us reshape almost any habit we have.

From Charles' point of view, the habit-loop has three common elements: cue, routine, and reward. They are forming a closed habit-loop together to meet the craving for a particular reward. For example, when every morning you get up and see the beautiful running shoes as your cue, and it naturally reminds you of the reward which could be anything that could satisfy the cravings your endorphins or a sense of accomplishment, then you can quickly start a routine of running. Every time you see the running shoes which you put in a very prominent place the night before, you will automatically get into the routine without any cost. Assuming that you are getting too old to run and want to change the habit from running to playing taijiquan, as long as you can identify the routine, experiment with rewards, and isolate the cue, you can have a plan to create a new habit of playing taijiquan by replacing the existing routine of running. In this way, Charles insists that, although it is difficult and time-consuming to change, you can finally manage to create your new habit if you don't give up.

Habit is determined both by nature and by nurture.

Just like you have a unique biological gene by nature, you have your own incomparable social gene which is your habit. By nurture, the habit is formed throughout your lifetime, and the way you think and act is based on upbringing, values, attitude, context or space they perceive yourselves in. Because no one is perfect in life, everyone has more or less developed good or bad habits like this or that. They are biologically inherited from your genealogy and socially determined by institutional context. Once formed, it is challenging for you to break it because of its stickiness and inertia. You cannot get rid of your habit. Instead, you can only create a new habit to replace it. Just think about how difficult it is to change the gene you have inherited from your parents, and you will know how hard it is to change your good or bad habits. Because of this, I can't agree more with how Charles Duhigg classifies the habit into three different levels: Individual habit, organizational process, and social institutions.

Among them, some profoundly rooted habits are so complicated that you cannot identify the cues or even the rewards of them. What makes the matter worse, some brains don't expect any reward from their life that no cravings for a happy and meaningful life can be aroused. While other brains struggle to climb Maslow's hierarchy of needs through their continuous efforts, but their hearts were not fully satisfied by merely moving from one level to the next linearly throughout their lives. The character and lifestyle that are determined by native families or institutional context sometimes constrain one's ability to see the most fundamental craving for a happy and meaningful life now.

The reason lies in a possible paradox between structure and agency that we have discussed in CHAPTER SPACE & CONTEXT. Now that your thoughts and behaviors are determined by space and context, how can you freely decide a cue or reward that can help you jump out of the existing habit-loop structure which conversely defines your decision-making behaviors? In other words, since your cognitive capacity and willingness to act are constrained mainly by institutional context, any decision you make cannot change the habit that has been imprinted by institutional properties. As a result, you can only have a craving within the context of your current "material" and "social" conditions. However, as you have learned from CHAPTER SPACE & CONTEXT, it just doesn't help to move aimlessly from one routine (cube) to another if you don't see the ultimate and constant craving for your life that is not constrained by your biological genes and the institutional context you are embedded in.

Now, you have *the Art of Life*, an open closed-loop which helps you transform every element of your habits: the cues, the routines, and, most importantly, the cravings. Only by returning to zero, can you see the primary meaning and your secondary meanings of your life by drawing your Identity Map. By designing your priorities, you could have a constant craving for a happy and meaningful life, as well as cravings for different needs that are connected with your identity at various life stages.

In this sense, *the Art of Life* is the keystone habit of creating new habits.

From Being to Transforming, you need to stop and return to zero by Being with *The Being*, and you begin to see the primary craving and secondary cravings. When you see your priorities and the never-ending engine, you may have the courage to take some critical actions. When you act consistently to meet those cravings, you can create a new habit. When you create your new habits, you will achieve your goals or have good virtues. With goals achieved and good virtues, you will continuously transform and grow. When you continually transform and grow with the golden spiral, your life is bound to be both happy and meaningful no matter what circumstances you are in.

To master the keystone habit of *the Art of Life* from Being to Transforming, you need an intellectual, experiential, and spiritual awareness to study and practice it in your daily life.

One of the good examples is Benjamin Franklin's thirteen virtues. In 1726, at the age of 20, Benjamin Franklin developed a "plan" for regulating his future conduct. He followed the plan he created "pretty faithfully" even to the age of 79 (when he wrote about it), and Benjamin Franklin was even more determined to stick with it for his remaining days because of the happiness he had enjoyed so far by following it. Benjamin Franklin committed to giving strict attention to one virtue each week, so after 13 weeks Benjamin Franklin moved through all 13. After 13 weeks he would start the process over again so in one year he would complete the course a total of 4 times. Benjamin Franklin tracked his progress by using a little book of 13 charts. At the top of each table was one of the virtues. The charts had a column for each day of the week and thirteen rows marked with the first letter of each of the 13 virtues. Every evening he would review the day and put a mark (dot) next to each virtue for each fault committed to that virtue for that day. Without such consistent perseverance and virtues, Benjamin Franklin could not be able to have so many achievements during his short lifetime.

Besides Benjamin Franklin, the resolutions of Jonathan Edwards and *Chuanxilu* by Wang Yangming are another two outstanding examples who cultivated their good keystone habits and virtues through resolutions and constant practice. Models cannot be limited to only these three people, because Charles Duhigg has already provided us numerous examples of how good habits can fundamentally transform some people's lives, as well as their brains.

Again, the template for your daily practice is provided below. I wish you could use this every day to create your keystone habit of *the Art of Life*.

PRACTICAL GUIDE FOR CREATING YOUR KEYSTONE HABIT

BEING: Start every morning with a quiet time; Complete this

template with meditation and pray so that you are Being with *The Being*;

SEEING: Find five critical activities within the following five categories and stages;

For example, Body, Mind, and Spirit (Being: meditation, pray, and taijiquan); Differential Relationships (green: wife); First Things First (red: write); Keystone Habit (yellow: writing); Virtue (blue: honesty);

DOING: Write down and visualize the specific tasks of these activities today; Keep healthy body, mind, and spirits, do meaningful things, build meaningful relationships, create your keystone habit, and cultivate your virtues;

ROUTINIZING: Keep doing these key activities every day, and never give up until you completely master *the Art of Life* and integrate it into your life;

TRANSFORMING Every night before going to bed, reflect over the day with a very short diary and give feedback on these activities; Have a sound sleep and start another brand new day.

TIME & NOW:

How to Live Every Moment of Your Life?

Yesterday is history, tomorrow is a mystery, today is God's gift, that's why we call it the present.

- Joan Rivers

Humans are hard-wired to anticipate and plan for the future; hence it is difficult for people to focus on the present as regards their future. Fortunately, when I began to deliberate on this topic and the whole book, I have the habit of walking. I am walking to work and home, and I immersed myself in living every moment of walking. When I walk, I can be in a flow to be free from anything that could influence me and gives me a sense of fully living in the now. In other words, I can be in *The Being* by praying, meditating, and breathing all the way through, and then I can see something that I could not see clearly during my busy day.

As for the topic of how to live the power of now, you might have already heard of Eckhart Tolle, the author of the Power of Now. You can either read his book or watch his YouTube video clips to understand the fundamental tenets of his thoughts. I will briefly introduce some points here by quoting his book in the following several paragraphs.

Why do you have to live every moment of your life?

The question has a close relationship with the topic of CHAPTER SPACE & CONTEXT. As has been mentioned in the chapter, you are living in so many different cubic blocks symbolizing a particular space or institutional context, and you are so deeply ingrained in this cube that you are nowhere to hide, and nowhere to run. Nobody can escape from such a constraint of time and space. Therefore, the purpose of living a life beyond these cubes while you live within is the main reason why you have to live every moment of your life as a human being with freedom.

From the teaching of Eckhart Tolle, we can have a lot of insights into the power of now. When you are facing problems, incidents, and challenges, once you have schemed your own solutions, you begin to give some labelings to all the related subjects. Within your own frame, you cannot extricate yourself. Because of this, In fact, you have always been under the control of your brain or mind, living in perpetual anxiety about time. You can't forget the past, and in the meantime, you habitually worry about the future. But in fact, you can only live in the present. Everything is happening in the present, and the past and future are just a hypothetical concept of time. That's why Joan Rivers said the following classic quote: Yesterday is history, tomorrow is a mystery, today is God's gift, that's why we call it the present. By subjecting to now, you can find real strength and access to peace and tranquility. There you can find real joy and embrace your true self.

According to the Power of Now, human beings feel pains and anxieties because they are firmly controlled by their own thinking and brains. In other words, human beings have become slaves to their own thinking. This habit of thinking itself as a kind of existence, and identifying with the wrong habit of thinking makes almost all people live in a "crazy and complex world full of problems and conflicts." What's more, we never let our brains rest. Through continuous learning, people can further create a false self by creating a series of concepts, labels, intentions, words, judgments, and definitions through identification with thinking, which hinders you from building all meaningful relationships. How to get rid of this kind of identification with thinking, and take the most critical step towards enlightenment? This book gives us two different ways:

The first method is to become an "objective observer", from identifying with your thoughts to being in the presence of *The Being*, that is, mindless and ego-less state; the second method is to transcend the excessive and compulsive thinking, focus on the present, and learn to be genuinely in a presence state. The first method is the spirits of STAGE ONE SEEING, the second method coincides with STAGE INFINITY TRANSFORMATION.

What I want to make clear is that I don't want to create another concept, label, pattern, or idea that put you trapped in another cubic block. The unique structure from *the Art of Life* itself reflects an open closed-loop that spirals upward, and you will understand the reason why THE STAGE ZERO BEING is included in *the Art of Life* but excluded from the main structure. So, to fully live every moment of your life, you have to keep *the Reader's Guide* in mind and learn to live within the presence of *The Being* here and now.

By nature, your whole life has a similar pattern with a day, and whether you can live a day determines whether you can live a happy and meaningful life or not. Sunrises like giving birth to a new life. As a matter of fact, you can make every moment of your life as a brand new beginning of your life as long as you can return to *The Being*. After seeing the current vision based on the meaning of your life with your Identity Map, you have to put it into action on the day, neither yesterday nor tomorrow. And the act of doing meaningful things and building meaningful relationships can be routinized into your habits. At night, you assume that you are facing your death with the sunset, and I hope you could be satisfied with all the things and relationships you have done this day no matter whether they are perfect or not. Just as you can say before going to bed every night: I had a happy and meaningful day, you can also tell when you finish your life: I had a happy and meaningful life.

In this way, you can practice living today as your last day. Based on such kind of practice, you can be in a status of awakening, and make every choice to fulfill the central purpose of your life.

The Art of Life is a new knowledge that is beyond the east and west. Since it is a new knowledge system, it is in the process of forming and has many flaws. And I hope you will not lose the very precious spirits of *the Art of Life*, without influenced by limited languages and expressions.

The Call here is to identify the meaning of your own life anytime, anyplace within *The Being*. Based on the purpose of your Being and Transforming as-is and to-be, you need to figure out what is the most important thing, people and time. As Tolstoy once suggested:

"Remember then: there is only one time that is important – now! It is the most important time because it is the only time when we have any power. The most necessary person is the one with whom you are, for no man knows whether he will ever have dealings with anyone else: and the most important affair is to do that person good, because for that purpose alone was man sent into this life."

Great comes from ordinary. Many great undertakings or achievements are accumulated through careless trifles. So is the nature of human society. In ordinary life, some people are either ordinary or excellent, while others are mediocre and inactive.

Tolstoy's remarkable teaching also reminds me of this ordinary nanny street photographer, Vivian Maier, because I will never forget the inspiration and touching that such an "ordinary" life once brought to me. Babysitter and street photographer, two seemingly unrelated professions, are perfectly integrated into Vivian Mayer's ordinary, hermit-like life. Apart from being a nanny, her only "thing" may be in the street, through her own lens and unique perspective, leaving ordinary people's happiness and sadness that are unnoticed by the public. She, herself, also completely and perfectly concealed her life from people's sight and fully lived her best living in an ordinary and dedicated way.

As a result, even those who employed her as a nanny knew that she had such a hobby, but they did not find her tremendous legacy in photography and kept her relics as "garbage." It wasn't until 2007 that a young collector, John Maloof, bid a box full of negatives for only $380 to write a history book. Since Vivian Mayer left no clues or traces for us to find out about her, all the legendary stories about her began slowly with the curiosity and inadvertent discovery of such a young collector.

The documentary, *Finding Vivian Maier*, released in 2013, gave us a vivid picture of all her remaining stories. I believe that after watching this documentary, there may be more mysteries about her life. We are not sure if we could understand such a unique experience and an independent soul, but I believe that such an effort, which seeks Vivian Mayer's ordinary life, will give us the greatest inspirations to live our lives now. It will also enable you to use an ordinary heart, open another regular, but a great day of your own life.

Let us declare that when all thoughts have fallen asleep, let Love be present.

PRACTICAL GUIDE FOR LIVING EVERY MOMENT OF YOUR LIFE

BEING: Be in the presence of *The Being*; meditate, pray, and breathe to empty everything in your mind; make yourself simple, pure, and free from every concept or thought that binds you;

SEEING: See that you sometimes become a slave of your own thinking habit; find your inner peace and calmness to feel the presence of *The Being* and now;

DOING: Return to zero, and accept all creatures as they are, and find their meanings as they are created to be and called to be, including your life;

ROUTINIZING: Create a habit of returning to zero; Constantly breaking the wrong habit of thinking by Being genuinely in the presence of *The Being*;

TRANSFORMING: When all thoughts have fallen asleep, let Love be present.

STAGE INFINITY

OUT OF THREE, THE CREATED UNIVERSE

Out of Tao, One is born; Out of One, Two; Out of Two, Three;
Out of Three, the Created Universe.

- Tao Te Ching, Chapter 42

In the beginning, God created the heavens and the earth. Now
the earth was formless and empty, darkness was over the
surface of the deep, and the Spirit of God was hovering over
waters. And God said, "Let there be light," and there was light.

- Bible, Genesis 1:1~3

Out of Three, The Created Universe. INFINITY (∞) means
TRANSFORMING through an open upward spiraling closed-loop.
You may continuously return to zero to constantly renew your
life at any moment. You will start anew where everything ends
because where there is death, there is a new life.

CLOSED & OPEN:

How Transformation Occurs?

Optimus Prime: Sam, you risked your life to protect the Cube?

Sam Witwicky: No sacrifice, no victory.

Optimus Prime: If I cannot defeat Megatron, you must push the Cube into my chest. I will sacrifice myself to destroy it. Get behind me. [Sam does so] It's you and me, Megatron!

- Movie, *"Transformers"*

The reason why I love to use science fiction movies or ethical dramas and animations to illustrate the abstract concepts is that they are dealing with all these cutting-edge topics and questions with great metaphors, symbols, and analogies in a more intuitive and visualized way.

Transformers, a series of American science fiction action films, also use the Cube, AllSpark, as a constant physical form that remains common across the multiverse which is capable of creating a new transforming life. However, any metaphor, symbol, analogy, or image created cannot fully explain *The Being* of all creatures: *Absolute Tao* or *I Am Who I Am*. That's why *the Art of Life* reminds you for the risk of being trapped in any cubic block, including *the Art of Life* itself.

No sacrifice, no victory.

This message is the answer to the question of how transformation occurs from the movie, Transformers. It's that simple, no big deal. It strongly echoes another well-known proverb: no pain, no gain, which implies every single small win in your life comes from your hard work and even painful work. That's why anyone who strives to achieve excellence is required to endure physical suffering and mental stress along the progress.

The problem is that everyone knows such a simple truth, but few people can really do it. That is to say, everyone wants to succeed, but no one wants to pay a real price for it. Albert Einstein is widely credited to define this kind of discrepancy between expectations and realities with his saying, "the definition of insanity is doing the same thing over and over again and expecting different results." Einstein used this definition of the word, insanity, to give a profound warning to those who live in their regular everyday lives. If you don't jump out of your regular comfort cube to make a difference in the things and the way you do every day, you will never get the different result from your life.

However, as has been mentioned in CHAPTER SPACE & CONTEXT and CHAPTER MATTER & HABIT, human beings, with a biological gene, are born to be embedded in a social routine. This is the biggest challenge for a person to transform his or her life.

To fill the gap between SEEING and DOING, *the Art of Life* bridges the isolated "material" and "social" dimensions by defining the habit as a set of routines of activities, which imbricate both technology and social behaviors. Social behaviors of a human being constitute social habit diachronically, while institution, as a social habit, constrains personal action synchronically. By incorporating the institutional context in which our human decision-making habits are embedded, *the Art of Life* addresses the dual roles of institutional pressures on forming a personal habit. The three institutional forces, which you have learned from CHAPTER SPACE & CONTEXT, coercive, normative, and mimetic pressures, not only influence the institutionalization of human activities respectively but are also inextricably intertwined together in the constitution of institutional contexts to affect the extent to which a personal habit can be formed.

The institutional context that is enacted and created through a process of attention influences a person's decisions and actions only when it is perceived by the person. On the one hand, the higher pressures you perceive from these institutional forces, the better you can reinforce your existing habit; on the other side, the higher the perception of mimetic pressures form the potential conflicts of patterns between different levels and units, the higher chance of transforming your habit and life. Generally speaking, coercive and normative forces will play a role to reinforce the formation of the existing practice, while mimetic pressures will play a pivotal role to create a new habit that could replace the existing one.

Knowing and perceiving the dual roles of institutional pressures from a rational perspective will significantly help you to understand how transformation occurs in your life. If habits are so firmly rooted in taken-for-granted rules, norms, and institutions, and if those habits are so compelling to determine your thoughts and behaviors, then how can your life get transformed by creating new habits or reinforcing existing ones? To change your life, as has been discussed in CHAPTER MATTER & HABIT on how to create your keystone habit, you have to overcome the dilemma between structure and agency by continually returning to zero and being with *The Being*.

Now, let's see the transformation occurs in more detail.

Based on the great insights from a classic paper written by Myeong-gu Seo and Douglas Creed in *Academy of Management*

Review (2002), the way to overcome the central paradox will be addressed.

Habits socially constructed at different levels and scales can produce potential interpersonal, inter-organizational, and interlevel contradictions among people and social units. For example, when you are born into a family, despite biological inheritance from your parents, you will find so many conflicts with the way your parent thinks and behave.   When you begin to work in society, you will also see the significant gaps between the habits mainly formed within your family context and the habits of your colleagues, companies, norms, cultures, and social institutions. When you get married, your biological and social gene is entirely different from your spouse.

Before the contradictions, conflicts, discrepancies, and separation, you will face another "road diverged in the yellow wood": either change yourself conform to the other part or reform the other part so that it can meet your needs. In most cases, you are adapting to the other side to gain legitimacy and support. There are some who creatively innovate the way people think and behave. No matter what you choose, you will not be happy with the result because you will never escape from such an endless cycle between your habit and social institutions. To transform the sequence into a spiral, you need to SEE the primary meaning of your life by Being with *The*

Being. Based on the primary purpose, you, as a transformational agency, can perceive all the unmet needs aroused by all the contradictions at different levels and scales with your heart, and mobilize all your limited resources to achieve the secondary meanings of your life.

To be the transformational agency, you need to fear no pains, sacrifice, and even death. Only when you have the love, the light never dims nor fails, can you have the power to sacrifice yourself to be transformed into a new being. If you meditate on the rebirth of an eagle, transformation from a caterpillar into a butterfly, the birth of new baby, and any brand new day that break through the dawn, you will see that they are sharing the typical pattern of living a new life from the death of the old one.

As an institutionally embedded human agency, conform to the existing institutional structure by passively changing your habits or transform the institutional context by constantly transforming yourself by Being with *The Being*? It's up to you to make a choice. However, please keep it in mind that great things always begin from the inside, because if an egg is broken by an outside force, life ends; If broken by an inside force, life begins.

PRACTICAL GUIDE FOR MAKING TRANSFORMATION OCCURS

BEING: Be in the presence of *The Being*; Meditate on the examples of typical transformation;

SEEING: See where everything begins, it will end; where it ends, it will start anew; perceive the potential conflicts and unmet needs of different stakeholders at different levels;

DOING: Transformation begins when you make a very tiny decision to start a new journey toward the new vision; need the courage to break the existing habit, rules, and norms from inside with love that never dims nor fails;

ROUTINIZING: Create a habit of finding and satisfying the unmet needs and opportunities; create a habit of reflections and transform your life from inside;

TRANSFORMING: Constantly return to zero, continuously transform every aspect of your life relationships, things, habits, and virtues.

LINEAR & NON-LINEAR:

How to Create a Golden Spiral in Your Life?

The good, of course, is always beautiful, and the beautiful never lacks proportion.

- Plato

Eadem mutata resurgo.

This Latine phrase which means "Though changed, I shall arise the same" was carved on the tombstone of a famous Swiss mathematician, Jakob Bernoulli (1654-1705). Although he wanted a logarithmic spiral, an Archimedean spiral was finally engraved. According to the book *E: Story of a Number*, authored by Eli Maor, Jacob was so moved by the discovery of "this marvelous spiral with such a singular and wonderful peculiarity" that he showed special awe for the golden spiral.

"... (it) always produces a spiral similar to itself, indeed precisely the same spiral, however, it may be involved or evolved, or reflected or refracted ... it may be used as a symbol, either of fortitude and constancy in adversity, or of the human body, which after all its changes, even after death, will be restored to its exact and perfect self."

- Jacob Bernoulli

The remarkable mathematical properties intrigued mathematicians, artists, and philosophers alike for centuries, and the logarithmic spiral, expressed in nature, architecture, art, design, music, and optimization, is used as a preferred growth pattern and a favorite motif of artistic design. You will be surprised by the universality and accuracy of the curve in which all structures, forms, and proportions grow and transform in the realms of both nature and art.

Let me give you a few simple examples. You will see the golden spiral in natural forms such as shells, horns, sunflowers, typhoons, and galaxies. You can also find the golden ratio expressed in human body proportions, in the arrangement of parts such as leaves and branches, and in artistic endeavors.

One of the approximations of the golden spiral is a Fibonacci spiral. Fibonacci sequence, named after Italian mathematician Fibonacci, is formed in a way that each number is the sum of two preceding ones, starting from 0 and 1. That is, (0,) 1, 1, 2, 3, 5, 8, 13, 21, 34, 44, 89, 144 and so on till infinity, and the ratio between the consecutive numbers of the sequence approaches the golden ratio as the numbers approach infinity,

The greatest truths are the simplest!

Although there are some other mathematical concepts, such as Fibonacci cubes or Fibonacci network, need to be further explored, 0, 1, 2, 3, and infinity is enough for you to understand the underlying connections between Fibonacci spiral and the golden spiral of *the Art of Life*.

As has been mentioned at the beginning of this book, a simple, elegant, and beautiful pattern is inspired by the core spirits of the two most influential books, the Bible and Tao Te Ching. They are unfathomable enlightenment of the first three verses from the book of Genesis in the Bible and one of the key verses from Tao Te Ching: Out of *Absolute Tao*, One is born; Out of One, Two; Out of Two, Three; Out of Three, the Created Universe. The patter has been translated into the following five stages of forming and transforming: Being, Seeing, Doing, Routinizing, and Transforming. These five stages are corresponding to the following numbers, concepts, and shapes: 0, 1, 2, 3, ∞; *Absolute Tao*, one, two, three and all things; and point, line, surface, cube, and hypercube, etc.

This is not a coincidence. The original pattern shared by nature, art, and spirituality converges on these initial numbers, and it is perfectly embodied in the body, mind, and spirit of a human being without any noise or loss. The growth pattern of your life resonates with this most basic creative model, and it provides a possibility that you could create the golden spiral in your life. The direction and locus of your life on this beautiful curve will help you achieve not only your personal happiness but also the social meaning of your life in a completely different way.

For this purpose, we have been learning these numbers, concepts, and meanings of these metaphors all the way through this small book, and they are forming the most basic and fundamental constituent unit that remains partially or wholly in all the creatures of this world, including the human beings.

Just as the physical cube, as the most constant physical form, can be transformed into any other physical shape, the individual human being, with a vibrating heart, is the most elementary constituent of this dynamic world. From this point of view, human beings can also be compared to cubes that have beating hearts. Based on this analogy, human beings are the prisoners of false cubic self which has been formed by concepts, labels, intentions, words, judgments, and definitions through identification with thinking in a particular institutional context. The cubes you have learned in CHAPTER SPACE & CONTEXT is actually yourselves, and the mission of the major characters in the movie actually implies a process of breaking out of your self, returning to zero, and being with *The Being*.

To make the process happy and meaningful progress, you have

to know the way how to create a golden spiral in your life.

In CHAPTER CHAOS & PRIORITIES, your whole life span has been involved to the day, and even the moment you live now and here. As long as you are being with *The Being*, you could find the meaning and priorities of your life. With the never-ending engine, love, you can surf on the curve of your golden spiral or dance with the vibrating rhythm of life from *The Being*.

The golden spiral also allows the organism to grow without changing shape, which implies that you don't have to change your Being as long as you are being with *The Being*. You are now a constant Being with *The Being*, and you accept yourself as it is created to be and as it is called to be at once. In other words, if you are on the right track with *The Being*, you can feel safe and happy at any moment of your life and enjoy every moment of your life. That's why *the Art of Life* advises: "If you know *The Being* and know yourself, you will have a happy and meaningful life whatever circumstances you are in."

Everyone has a unique golden spiral, and you need to see it with your heart. At any point on the curve, the tension of two directions between involving or evolving, introspection or outrospection, and life and death are One only when you are with *The Being*. Again, the better you know *The Being*, the better you will know yourself; and the better you know yourself, the better you will see *The Being*.

Life is as natural as you breathe. Inhale to life exhale to death, and grow with the golden spiral. The simple, elegant, and beautiful growth pattern of nature can also be your life growth pattern, as long as you completely master all the five stages of *the Art of Life*, which together constitute an open closed-loop that spirals with the golden ratio.

The golden spiral with golden ratio presents us a sustained life growing path with optimized size and locus which permeates all structures, forms, and proportions. Among them, your happy and meaningful life matters most, because only when you create a golden spiral in your life with *The Being*, you can connect all those missed links and create sustained growth, and even to infinity.

We don't know how the universe created out of three with a golden spiral, but you can feel how a small idea spirals and changes the world from the movie, *Pay It Forward (2000)*.

Assignment: Think of an idea to *CHANGE* our world - and put it into *ACTION*!

Idea: It's me, and that's three people.

               And I am going to help them,

               but it has to be something really BIG.

Something they can't do by themselves.

So, I do it for them.

Then, they do it for three other people,

that's nine, and they ...

- The Movie, *"Pay It Forward"*

PRACTICAL GUIDE FOR CREATING A GOLDEN SPIRAL IN YOUR LIFE

BEING: Return to zero, empty your mind, be formless, shapeless;

SEEING: See the world, as a grand living organic, shares a common growing pattern that spirals; see *the Art of Life* is forming an open closed-loop which spirals with golden spiral;

DOING: Determine your optimized activity size between who you know (relationships) and what you do (things), between tacit knowledge and explicit knowledge; focus on the meaning of your life, and don't pursue excessive profits or ambitions; Dynamically find the golden ratio between all the dual structure such as market and hierarchy, zero and one, wave and particle to achieve the optimized size;

ROUTINIZING: Create a habit of finding the optimized size of your life so that you could grow with an optimized path which forms a golden spiral in your life; optimized size determines sustainable growth along the optimized path;

TRANSFORMING: Constantly return to zero to start a new loop that will create a golden spiral in your life.

MACRO & MICRO:

Your Happy and Meaningful Life Matters!

Things being investigated, knowledge became complete. Their knowledge being complete, their thoughts were sincere, their hearts were then rectified. Their hearts being rectified, their persons were cultivated. Their persons being cultivated, their families being regulated. Their families being regulated, their states were rightly governed. Their states being rightly governed, the whole kingdom was made tranquil and happy.

-Zengzi, *The Great Learning (Daxue)*

That was a gloomy rainy day twenty years ago when I was a junior at the University.

I, with heavy footsteps, was walking along the crooked road by the campus lake with the most profound sorrow in my heart. It was the end of the world to me. Growing up in a completely broken family, I only wish to have an intact family either through the reunion of my divorced parents or by setting up my own happy family. Naturally, a happy family became my only purpose in life for which I was prepared to do anything to achieve it.

The hope helped me survive from the tragedies of my childhood. From seven years old, I began to steal, smoke and wander from place to place. My childhood was full of sneers, sorrow, hunger, separations, and transfers but I didn't despair because I had a dream.

To make a dream come true, ever since middle school, I began to read all the psychological, biographical and self-help books in the nearby library. I naively thought my parents would reunite if I succeeded in self-healing and getting admission into a top-tier University.

After six years of hard work, I was accepted into Peking University, one of the top Universities in China but nothing happened. Then I decided to build my own, but the girl whom I loved said goodbye. It was the last straw. I felt lost and dead at that moment. Nothing is more lamentable than a dead heart where time stops. But in that moment of my despair, I began to SEE my life from a completely different perspective.

That may be paradoxical, but it did happen in my life. I don't have to be perfect to live a happy and meaningful life because every moment of life including the suffering of childhood is beautiful. No one had such an enriched life like I turned out to have and everything I experienced is my wealth that I cannot be deprived of.

I began to see my life as it is and I fell in love with it again. From that moment, I started an entirely new experience of renewing my dreams, my love, and my life. Along the journey, I had two great teachers: one is my continuously dramatic life adventures, and the other is knowledge gleaned from the books I read as well as multi-level, multi-cultural and inter-disciplinary researches I did in the Universities.

Twenty years later, I am now not only living the meaning of my life but also helping people to live better, happier and meaningful lives. I am also living happily with the girl who had left me twenty years ago, the girl whom I love most, parenting two beloved daughters.

I think it is time to share my limited but useful insights and inspirations with people to whom it might be helpful. This is how the book, *the Art of Life* came into being. As you can see, this is my personal story from zero to one, from nothing to something, from emptiness to meaning. Not to mention those big gurus in our times, if you take some time to observe any ordinary people around you who are living a happy and meaningful life, you will find that they all have similar stories to tell.

Now it is your turn to live and tell your own stories because your happy and meaningful life really matters.

No one can substitute your role in transforming your habits and life. That's why *the Art of Life* has to be achieved and written together with your extensive involvement. Every tiny action in every moment of your life is influenced and further influence the cubic block you are living in. No one knows what your current situation is, what is the primary meaning of your life, and what are your priorities right now, and the only thing you can do is to see them by returning to zero and doing it exceptionally well. By making the extremely great action into your keystone habit, your life will definitely make a difference.

Finally, I hope you enjoy *the Art of Life* and live a happy and meaningful life now and here.

PRACTICAL GUIDE FOR LIVING A HAPPY AND MEANINGFUL LIFE

BEING: Meditate, pray, breathe to empty everything in your mind, make yourself simple, pure, and free from anything that binds you. Recover your inner peace and calmness by Being in the presence of *The Being*.

SEEING: See the simple, elegant, and beautiful pattern: *the Art of Life;* see *the Art of Life* as a keystone habit that creates new habits; See *the Art of Life* as a pattern imprinted in all creatures.

DOING: Study and practice what you have learned. Know *Absolute Tao* and *I Am Who I Am* more. Live beyond *the Art of Life*;

ROUTINIZING: Apply *the Art of Life* to every moment of your life daily, weekly, monthly, yearly, and your whole life; Finally, you don't need *the Art of Life* to live a happy and meaningful life;

TRANSFORMING: Just enjoy your happy and meaningful life. Period.

DID YOU ENJOY THE ART OF LIFE?

Thank you so much for purchasing and reading this small book.

If you enjoyed the adventure with *the Art of Life*, I would like to ask you a favor to leave me a special review on Amazon.

I do appreciate it if you tell me how you applied *the Art of Life*, a simple, elegant, and beautiful pattern, to solve your real-life problems.

I am also ready to get any comments or feedback from my readers, and your thoughts will be a great help to make this small book grow with a golden spiral. Please visit machmic.com and contact me anytime you like.

Thanks again, and I am looking forward to hearing your voice and thoughts soon.

Minghao (Michael) Huang

33265874R00069

Made in the USA
San Bernardino, CA
20 April 2019